The poetry of Erik Dana Davidkov is shot through with music, silence and silver. At times I felt as if I were a witness to a stranger's dreaming. It moved me.

- Anthony Reynolds

What's distinctive in Erik Davidkov's poems is his felt presence. He doesn't just observe, as poets do, but also allows us to observe him, honestly. Him and those close to him, his family, friends, and painters he admires. He shows us, in his own phrase, *how to invest in someone else.*

— A.C.H. Smith

LEVIATHAN

Signed by Erik Davidkov

March 23, 2023

~~ERIK DAVIDKOV~~

~~LEVIATHAN~~

NEW & SELECTED POEMS
2015-18

Dedicated to friends and enemies.

LEVIATHAN

The past is the one thing we are not prisoners of.
We can do with the past exactly what we wish.
What we can't do is to change its consequences.

— **John Berger**

No tree, it is said, can grow to heaven unless its roots reach down to hell.

— **C.G. Jung**

LEVIATHAN

NEW & SELECTED
POEMS
2015-18

A PLACE WHERE WE CAN MEET

After months of spending time together,
I noticed you changed the way you laugh,
it sounded a lot like mine, mimicking
the highest and lowest pitches.

It became apparent that we had adapted
our mannerisms, rather selfishly,
we echoed each other,
even in our pathetic little talks.

We would talk about politics, right and left,
our views had contrasted, but now met
somewhere around the wrong middle,
and we started going backwards.

We didn't have the time to agree
on how much of yourself you leave
and how much of me you take,
we just assumed and took what was left.

Then we both became mute,
but only for each other, left in the aftermath,
a silence, limited to our ears only,
at first unnoticeable, then unbearable.

It's like taking a hike to our favorite spot
and seeing a hole where the lake used to be.

When you spoke of the Sun, warmth and flowers,
your face would light up and reflect the shine onto me.
Let's talk about something as boring as the weather,
and the weather is beautiful today.

SACRIFICE

Because they wanted us to learn
life is difficult after school is over,
after exams and doodles
on desks and papers,
the responsibilities came about,
because now the kid's grown up,
there are new things to understand,
like how to invest in someone else
so that you can love and feel
for someone other than yourself.

    As a child, you wrote with a graphite,
    but now, replaced by ink,
    it becomes more difficult
    to erase the mistakes you make.

FRANKIE MACHINE

The man with the golden arm
walks up to you in the crowded room
and kindly asks you to light his cigarette
and as he inhales to light, both hands shake.

He is hurting, there is something hidden
behind this unbearable heaviness of being,
a state of mind left after the change had come.
He is a different animal - from the skinny build
you can see that both his shadow and silhouette
are variations of the same broken person.

You ask Otto about this man.
He replies - *There's a great tragedy*
in any human who gets hooked on something,
whether it's heroin or love.
The man with the golden arm sits next to you
and whispers in your ear – *It leaves nothing else*

to be desired.

WHAT GOD INTENDED
for Vera, Vladimir and Dmitri Nabokov

If I said I was a martyr,
would you kneel and pray for me?

If I said I was forgiveness,
would you heal the rest of me?

If you said I was a liar,
would I keep your faith in me?

If you said I was a memory,
would you still be there for me?

If I said he was my child,
would you see his eyes in me?

If I said he was forgiveness,
would you cry with him for me?

If my voice became the wind,
would you still pretend to breathe?

If the devil sought forgiveness,
if it all came back for me,
if it all came back to haunt you,
if it all came haunting me.

If we hadn't just pretended,
that it all became forgiveness,
if it's all what God intended,
would you still remember me

CADMIUM RED
after John Berger and John Christie

For no better reason than to remind you of flowers,
I send you cadmium red. It is the same color
of, say, when you were a child looking at the sky,
closing your eyes, seeing the blood in your eyelids,
that red, not violent as it can sometimes be,
but innocent, illuminated through the skin.

And say you opened your eyes, saw your grandfather
throwing a colorful ball for you to catch.
You were on a beach, or maybe in a forest,
where nothing is better than bad weather.
Your grandfather is younger, picking up flowers,
piece by piece; broken petals on lonely ground.

Then you saw the bees pollinating and one of them
landed on your hand, stung a crucifix into your skin.
He flicked it away, *go, go and pollinate elsewhere*,
the pain closed your eyes and now, now it's over,
he is no longer there, nor are the bees, no, you have grown
now,
for the time being, you are leaping over red petals,

much like that ritual he told you about when you were a kid,
where father and son, barefoot, dance over embers that radiate
intense amounts of heat long after the fire has been extinct,
somewhere in ancient Greece, or Thrace, where cadmium red,
in the form of a flower, lies on top of a cold, forgotten monolith.

REMEMBER, BODY
for Luis Buñuel

when you were held and passed around,
when nothing really mattered,
and everything you felt was new, remember

when your body tingled,
as your mother hummed the song
that became your own, remember

when you first drew blood,
how it dripped like honey,
remember, body, remember

when you held a hand,
how different it felt to all other hands,
because you loved another body, remember

when you were stretched, tattooed,
how nails scratched your back,
because of passion, remember

when you went inside another body,
to plant bad seeds, leave, then come back,
how it felt to love, body, remember

when you heard your song in a dream,
stored in the subconscious, your mother's voice,
how much you need her, remember

when you were old, lost all memory,
a vaudeville act with no trunk,
how sexless & careless you were, remember

when harvesting teardrops,
you dreamed about leaping over heaps of sleeping children,
praying you could move again, remember

when they prepared you for the dirt nap,
with velvet cushions around you,
and soil knocked hard on wood, remember

when you were laid to rest,
trapped in amber, surrounded by few,
who will forever hum your song, remember

when the song became an echo,
when they never came back,
when all feeling had gone,
when you stepped away,
and let the world turn

remember body,
remember
you're dead
longer than you are alive

THE GOSPEL ACCORDING TO MOTHER

Smoking her cigarette, ashes falling on the carpet,
my mother would lay next to me in bed,
and tell me a story that her mother told her
when she was young and sleepless.

The gospel according to her mother was that
God created the planet without deserts,
and for every sin that man commits
a peck of sand would fall on the ground.

This isn't really a bedtime story, she'd say,
just something interesting I remembered.

AND MATTER
ON DOMINION DAY

Sometimes the caterpillar stays in the cocoon
longer than it needs to. Maybe because it's difficult
changing into something completely different,
something new. Maybe it is comfortably numb
in the state between its last breath as one thing
and its first one as the next. Maybe it is the fear
of saying goodbye to what it knows best.

Much like people, living in a shell of own,
studied in biology classes on *fig. 1* and *fig. 2*,
bodies, living, breathing, striving for the ~~ubermensch~~,
constant neuro-klepto-manifestation of the self,
constant replacement of cells, hairs, skin,
maybe it is to do with sadness and nostalgia
and the way it affects the human brain,
but much like caterpillars, people are afraid
of goodbyes to the known, the own, the shell.

The last people – the idiots, the sick, the insane
and matter –
They don't have to live their lives
being afraid of goodbyes.

Chances are the goodbyes are never going to stop.

HOW HIGH DOES THE SYCAMORE GROW?
ON PATRIMONY

part i (1999) noli me tangere[1]

As a child, at the beginning of every summer,
I would request that my grandfather show me where
the sycamore tree I planted was.

I would be told that it hasn't left the soil yet,
the cars that hover over it one way, flatten it out the other,
breaking it down, to just an inch of stem and roots.

I remember, grandfathers white horse would prefer to lay
exactly where I planted the sycamore seed,
more than any other place on our land.

As time passed and as landscapes changed, winter came
and the elderly horse became immensely ill,
casting a shadow of a perfect death onto the white snow.

I pretended to be asleep, when I heard grandfather
walk down the steps, past the veranda, with a black blanket
over his shoulders, to put another blanket on the horse, as it
lay on top of my sycamore.

---

[1] *Noli me tangere* is the **Latin** version of a phrase spoken, according to **John 20:17**, by **Jesus** to **Mary Magdalene** when she recognized him **after his resurrection**. These three words can be translated in different ways: "do not touch me", "do not hold on to me", "do not approach me", and so on.

He would speak to it, I couldn't hear it, as my window view
was muted, but it was comforting, as the horse would lick his
hand and push its face into his belly,
like a child seeking the comfort of its mother.

It seemed like they had agreed on something,
as my grandfather gave it a prolonged embrace, a kiss,
a gentle caress on its back, and a touch of heads.

He imagined an X between the horses' eyes and ears,
took a gun out and placed it on its forehead,
as the horse stayed motionless, grandfather closed his eyes.

Before I could close mine, it happened in seconds,
the horse fell on the snow, my grandfather fell to his knees,
grabbed the horse by the head and began to mourn.

The snow slowly turned red and the horse was left alone,
only covered by a black blanket and freshly fallen snow,
and in folklore, snow are angels collecting the spirit.

We didn't speak about it until much later.

part ii (2009) cancer absconditious[2]

My grandfather was making a pot of coffee,
as I was sketching the outline of a horse's head,
in red, on a white canvas,
I had dreamed of it the night before, in bright colors.

You start with the geometry first,
then you add details and begin shading, therefore the sketch
had a lot of circles and lines,
as the horse made its way home through the pencil.

To have the forehead symmetrically correct,
I had to draw a cross between where the ears and eyes would
be, then a line down from the middle of the eyes
to each nostril, then the mouth.

It looks a lot like him, you know, said my grandfather,
looks a lot like Graham. I was unaware of the name.

*I had to shoot him, you know, he was old,
I did him a favor.*

I know, I'd say, *I saw you do it,
not something I want to remember,
but my brain fought that memory last night, and it lost.*

And I tried forgetting this picture, of the horse falling,

---

[2] (on Nori me tangere) The words were also occasionally used to
describe a disease known to medieval physicians as a "hidden
cancer" or **cancer absconditus**, as the more the swellings
associated with these cancers were handled, the worse they
became.

my grandfather crying, this Mustang dying,
but the more I tried forgetting, the worse it became.

I still beg for his forgiveness every day and every night, he'd
say, *I had him since he was a baby,*
and when I shot, it took all his pain
and placed it on my shoulders.

Doing that felt like shooting myself in the foot,
then shooting myself in the knee, then in the stomach,
the chest, the throat and then the head.

I had heard that a shot like that could also disable the horse,
rather than kill it, I would have had to shoot again,
and that frightened me more than anything else.

He then suggested my painting be called
Death in a French Garden, or *Peril*,
in tribute to Graham from the film of the same name
who was shot in his own property, in the backyard.

He's was here before the house was built, so this property is
as much his as it is mine, he'd say, *and as he died where*
your sycamore was trying to break through,
I put a small wall of metal wires around it
to keep it from harm,

                                        and it grew, and it grew.

SOFIA/a late afternoon in winter
mid december, 2016

I.   Every city has its old woman, who either throws seeds to pigeons, or leftovers to dogs and is always kind to the children who walk by her.

II.   Every city has its old man, who sits on a bench in front of a bus stop, waiting for the driver who is never on time to take him to the village where he'd see his friends, old and new,   as obituaries stapled to trees.

III.   In the late afternoon, as if by a grand design, snow falls, like rags - heavy, shiny and peaceful.

IV.   In the late afternoon in winter, reminiscing of her childhood and what life was without the halo, God walks on the street and greets all the children and their snow angels.

V.   Every city has its own snow angels in winter. The old woman and man have made their mark, so did the pigeons, the dogs, the cows, the children and God herself.

VI.   Sofia becomes a snow angel every winter.
This winter is no different.

SAPIENS & HOMO DEUS
IN EXILE

I. THIS EXTINCTION EVENT

The sweet release of lead on an angel's face,
as the ass watches us, this fragile secretion,
to make the prayers even and God's peek
from their small metal boxes on the hill.

II. NARCISSUS POMPEII

The sweet release of lead into Earth,
as She moans and groans from ever volcano,
and rains on top of me, pleasuring me, cooling me,
as the bible rewrites itself and disappears completely.

III. THE BLACKOUT

The sweet release of lead into the pages of law,
the land is chaos, people believe in golden scripture,
as the orgasms of Earth smudge the writing off papyruses,
it's all over now, we need to discover fire again.

† THE SACRIFICE

Man paints a woman with charcoal inside a cave,
naked, wide open and her breasts abnormally large.
Then he puts the fire out and falls asleep.
In the morning, he wakes and touches his hard penis.
Philosophy presses against his veins, throbbing.
He looks at his painting, rubs the tip
and covers Her in lead

A SHIP RETURNING FROM A VOYAGE
IS NOT THE SAME VESSEL AS IT WAS ON
SETTING SAIL
after MARK SELIGER

After the bridge comes the mist,
after the mist, some rain must fall,
after the rain, the temperature changes.

Before the body collapses, the temperature changes,
before the mist, snow covers the bridge,
before the bridge, the body curves.

After the bird had died, it was included in the collection,
after the body fell, it was included in the collection,
before the spoilt fruit, came the worms.

Before the bird had died, it was never valued,
before the body fell, the collection wasn't even planned,
after the bridge was constructed, worms flew on mist.

Before the flood was photographed, it was cloudy.
After the curves of the body, the waves formed a woman.
Before her breasts turned to rock, her nipples turned to sand.

After she was laid on rocks, God caressed her hair.
Before the rock turned into sand, time became irrelevant.
After electricity was discovered, snakes sizzled in protest.

After the two boys met on the bridge, came the mist.
Before the pain, the ruin came, the ruin with a name.
After the mist, some rain fell, the temperature changed.

Before the city collapsed, the body curved.
After the stream of pain, the body steps on thin ice.
Before the temperature changed, the body was the same.

In between before and after was a pathway of rocks,
in the middle of a lake, which leads to the body of a woman.

Fruit sprouts in this woman, filled with worms and
oil, a soil lashed with lead and prone to disease, to infection.
A soil in which a bird will fly into, get a worm, then out.

If this woman floats with the current,
she will reach a way to prevent her pain.

If she decides to swim against it,
then she will perhaps reach the source.

LEAVING EARLY
after JOHN ASHBERY and HENNING MANKELL

I had a dream, two years before I left home,
about two brothers (by the end of the dream – one).

One held his limp penis in his left hand and lightly jerked it.
The other, reserved and blushing, held his eyes with his hand.

The first took all his clothes off and stepped into the shower.
The other couldn't wait for the steam curtain to appear.

The other left the room, sat and waited outside the door.
The first showered, then stepped out onto the cold floor.

The first opened the door and saw another door.
The other was expected, but absent.

The lone brother kept opening doors, but found no end.
He would go to his limp penis for advice.
His manhood could only assist in pleasure, not pain.

By the end of the dream, the brother was alone,
walking through doors, one after the other,
never coming to an end, and that's how it should be.

   Sinning isn't easy,
                    it's just very bittersweet.

TERRA NULLIUS[3]

There is nobody here, except for the woman with the hat,
and I leave my socks behind to join her in the water.

We meet halfway between the deep and shallow,
there is no sun, but moonlight, no heaven in sight.   ·

We move towards the reflection of Méliès moon,
it accepts us, naked, changing, swallows us whole.

Before she leaves, I want to bring the Sun back,
so that the day starts again, so that I enter again.

I can control the weather with my moods,
but I can't control my moods at all.

She knows this, then walks over to me,
tells me she is here until I erase her from the page.

I can control her story with my moods
but I can't control her with my moods.

This happiness won't last, I assume.
Happiness like this is highly unlikely,

I begin to accept reality. It cuts me up.

---

[3] Latin expression meaning *nobody's land*. For example, Australian aborigines had inhabited Australia for over 50,000 years before European settlement, which commenced in 1788. Indigenous customs, rituals and laws were unwritten. It has been claimed that Australia was considered terra nullius at the time of settlement.

MANY MANDARIN SKINS LATER

My childhood held the smell of white roses, half dead,
placed neatly in an empty Stolichnaya Vodka bottle,
with a centimeter of water at the gut
and a wool bow at the neck,

to keep the roses warm and fresh, my grandmother would say,
for them to have a reason to stay pretty, even though
they've been cut, for human consumption, she'd say,
for us to devour their beauty.

Whenever she watched T.V.
my grandfather would smoke a big cigar,
a cigar which only politicians smoked those days,
and I knew he wasn't, but if you didn't know him
and eavesdropped, you'd think otherwise,

like that time when he said that all hooligans should be shot for
disobeying the communist regime, then saying
how you don't hear of hooligans at all these days
because they're caught, beaten then killed.

Sometimes they would eat mandarins for dinner,
just that, the fruit, juicy little ball, as my grandfather called it,
with skin that smells divine once put on top
of the old Russian stove,
to sizzle, dry out and disappear.

Many mandarin skins later, I find myself alone,
in their room, peeling one, enjoying the juiciness,
in a cold room, where their obituaries radiate presence, through
the glass cabinet, where they used to leave

their glasses before sleep.

I place a few logs into the body of the stove
and set them on fire with an old news article
about how Gorbachev ended the cold war
and I watched as his face burned slowly.

I take the mandarin skins and put them on top the hot metal.

I take rose petals fallen on each side of the vodka bottle
and place them around the mandarin skins.

They sizzle, dry out and disappear.

PERCEPTION

We need to remind susceptible children
if they decide to copy the violence on T.V.
they must mirror their actions to be accurate.

THREE CONCLUSIONS
ON POWER, CORRUPTION AND LIES

Philosophy rubs against your penis,
ideals and ideology whet your appetite,
red and yellow, a sickle in the eye,
an assertion that if a wet painting is touched, it stains.

Relax, don't do it.

And where bibles used to stop bullets,
now its mobile phones and porn computers,
and deals with God, and she is here and always will be,
for some maybe not always,
but to believe in reincarnation
is to completely admit defeat.

Relax, don't do it.

After humans decide to fight one another
with more than fists and guns and nucl. weapons,
our successors, if any, would have to re-discover fire,
and as we were taught in school,
that took us quite a while.

Relax, it's already happening.

THE RABBIT SKINNER
after David Sylvian

I am the hunter, who runs like a hunted animal,
across roads, hoping that the light on my peripheral vision
is an orgy of fireflies, that, when penetrating each other,
they glow, with a blurry outline,
a white, impenetrable planet.
This song has been spinning since 1969, when a soldier, my
father, showed me a rifle & how to use it.
I am breathing, I am there, holding the rifle, aimed at a
rabbit's ear, to go through one and exit through the other.
I am there and, also, not there.

My father, a martyr in his own right, waiting
to hear the bang, to see if the rabbit
would run away or stay.

I shoot, and the noise renders me temporary deaf.

I am breathing, I can see my mother weeping.
I can see her mother weeping.
I shoot, but continuously look
at my father's face, which seems wet to touch.
Mother runs towards the rabbit,
rubs her wet hand onto its fur and lifts it.
And I run, out of guilt, lips too dry to speak or cry,
didn't need to talk, had no one to talk to anyway.

I have become the hunter,
running across roads like a hunted animal.

EARL GREY DAYS

I am the man in the apple, coat and hat
and the crescent moon hovering above.

I am Lou Reed, throwing cigarette buds at the stars,
while Laurie plays her violin to the dogs.

I am a gun, a bullet free pistollet, I click,
like a very agitated and ultraviolent cricket.

I pray like a mantis, looking at the stars, singing the pain.

My water with an earl grey bag, baptized in a black mug,
goes down my trachea, and spreads around my lungs
the feeling of warmth in the cold-near deceased body.

I must sleep now, I need to dream of Mary Lou
and if I don't, I'd rather not wake up.

THERE ARE THINGS I KNOW FOR CERTAIN
ABOUT PHOTOGRAPHS

~~scene 1~~
~~I sing to my mother at night~~
~~scene 3~~
~~the corner of our picture isn't creased~~
~~scene 4~~
~~angels like yours are made from paper and spit~~
~~scene 5~~
~~the people have voted~~
~~scene 6~~
~~this theatre is making me sick~~

############################*TELEKON*

in the background, a dog running across
a barb wired plot of land
with half its face out of frame
destination- unknown,
emotionally out of focus.

in the foreground, an old woman
standing next to a chair, dressed in white,
holding a rose, leaves ~~*me with only one thought*~~
~~*why don't you just sit the fuck down?*~~
me breathless, with my semi-automatic heart,
I look to the dog for inspiration, as the woman is obvious,
and I am only interested in what I do not fully understand.

MERCY IS OVERRATED

You've seen oceans dry,
and whole worlds come apart,
you've seen bridges fall,
now here you are, where darkness doubles.

You've woven parachutes out of broken memories,
out of grandad, mother, father, sister-
and you've felt so cold.

And God only allows you to love
the ones that don't want **your** love,
then the ones that **you** don't want to love.

And I know when you smile, something else is going on,
I know you disappear, when you sing the pain.

Now here we are, at war again,
where light pours in & darkness doubles,
where truth is an unknown pleasure,
where we are lost in translation,
and you feel so cold.

And we are lost.

GIMME SHELTER
is it honey, is it gold

Like reviewing the Zapruder film,
like reviewing Harvey Oswald's assassination tape,
like thinking of the past as an event
which should have never taken place,
between the violence and the ground,
sheep dressed like wolves and vice versa,
crazies expecting peace
through cut hair and bed-ins,
when for someone home is a question mark
and the poor remain poor,
and the rich question their advisors
if killing the poor is a viable option,
and if we could go back, we wouldn't,
because this is how it will always be,
if not now, in a hundred years,
the past desires to be immortal,
the future is immortality manifest,
the past dictates the future.

MACRORRHIZA[4]

Through the window, I see my mother, kneeling in the garden,
her hands, opened wide, in conversation with God,
among flowers, roses, daffodils, a baby cherry tree,
all of them, including mother, encased in dirt, the roots.

I walk to her. I kneel next to my mother, hear *voda, voda*.
This is a prayer for water. She is kindly asking for water.
Not from God, she holds no idols close,
but from Nature.

Nothing is better than bad weather. I surrender.

I see the sky, with its rain, dripping in my mouth,
like rain drips from a petal of a rose, onto its stem.
I touch the wet grass. It crackles between my fingers.
The sun is rising from the east. We are heliotropes.
I bury my feet into the soil, turn towards east.

I am a plant.[5]

---

[4] from Latin – a plant with large roots.

[5] this was once revealed to me in a dream

L'ACCORD BLEU
after Yves Klein

The sky is as blue as I want it to be,
And, if I choose to believe grandmother,
then grandfather is up there,
dressed like a king of the wild frontier
with blue paint stains on his hip.
He flips pork loins on a grill
and listens to Lennon and McCartney,
throws bones for the dogs to fetch,
still reading Henning Mankell's novel,
lying in a hammock, counting planes,
thinking about how, when I was little,
I threw a Rolling Stones' record out the window,
and how it decapitated a pigeon.
Then he'd be thinking of me
and when I'd come home.

72 HOURS

I
In Belgrade, we lie on the grass,
the two of us, naked, like animals
our skins touch, like sand and glue.
Beetles in my stomach, butterflies in yours.

II
In the Sava lake we swim for hours,
our hands acquire a sea creature-like texture.
I touch your back, you turn around.
We breathe in deep and dive.

III
We kiss for an hour, then you walk away

and look for somebody else to set on fire.

GOLDEN RATIO
an anfase of Katyusha

I have only seen it once, through the viewfinder
of your camera, and it was real, raw
and somewhat beautiful. Your curls, illuminated
by the red traffic light, your portrait -pale, freckled-
a smile not for my eyes, not this time, positioned
between the x and y, a symmetrical composition,
a tribute to Fibonacci. The backdrop – a wet Liverpool, of
     course, burned on my retina,
a 35mm negative of desire.

I often think of you
and where you will be on photographs.

EXPLAINING JOSEPH BEUYS
TO HIS DEAD HARE

The portrait is the grey felt suit.
It gives and receives emotion
and when nobody is looking
it moves and dances,
and translates poetry
in the wrong key.

LEVIATHAN

In your dreams you think you are invincible,
you can swim in the skies as you would in water,
you cannot be hooked, tamed or trapped,
and your mother always called you dangerous.
In reality, you are aware this is only in dreams,
you try to figure it out, but the questions never end,
and you are alone in the world, without family
or lust for life, a thought of comfort worries you.
As you walk on the beach, dry feet on wet sand,
you see yourself, washed up on the shallow,
a whale the size of your home times ten,
with every inch of life rotting away.
You let time pass, then visit the grave again,
now you have become a cathedral of bones.
You lay inside your ribcage, naked, alone,
listen to your body speaking, the song is empty.
Nothing can upset the balance of good and evil,
and your absolute submission is the path to freedom.
You walk away with the knowledge that this death
is somehow deserved and should not be questioned.
Now, knowing that the animal you dreamed of
is also mortal and can also die, you become humbler.
You are disappointed, and this trauma stays,
you begin to come apart at the seams.
You begin to dream of a black and blue void,
in which you dive, disappear and on the other side,
maybe, with selfless sacrifice and confidence,
you will be the Leviathan just for one more time.

QUIET RESOURCE

I have run out of love, hope and fear,
but I will take some from the past.

BLIND

Something called my name, as I was swimming
with a friend who I had never met, inside
a square pool that seemed to have no
bottom, only darkness. Something called
me to go outside. A soft voice, called out
my name, as if on a beach calling out into
the sea. *The sea is blind, but it can hear,
and how much it listens.*

As I stepped out of the pool, I saw my mother,
kneeling, calling out for me, pointing at
the same direction where many others
were carefully looking towards. I saw
cars, people, horse backed and barefoot,
children and animals running towards us
with savage speed. Nomads, depraved
animals, once a civilized people.

Behind them, the tower of Babel cracked and fell,
every stone of beautifully hand-crafted
art, fell to the ground. *Something is
chasing them*, I said, *we need to go.* The
tower, they say, the disciples rose for *her*,
and seeing the sun shine, as it fell
brought tears to our eyes.

God said it's all too dark, a woman turned around
and said, *he has seen the end, and it is
here, coming for us. Mother*, I said, *we
need to run*. My mother looked at me in a
way I have never seen before. She didn't
look sad, neither worried.

She has become an old woman, she cannot run, she
knew this was the end. She put both arms
around me, as did I. *I'm so cold*, I said,
don't leave me blind. You run, she said to
me calmly, *I'll stay, clean the house and
wait for you to come back home.*

~~LEVIATHAN~~

The custom officers at the border of your dreams
confiscate you and your ability to be a fish,
to swim without needing to breathe,
to not have a broken little heart,
forgive them, for they know what they are doing.

All two things you wanted more than anything,
taken from you, white as a ghost,
you are back to your powerless body, hungry, washed out
and this is only the beginning.

Jesus hears you crying, but isn't he crying too?
You surrender.

The skin on your ankles felt soft as you swam in the water,
but now the cleaners have stripped you naked
and placed back your chains, barcodes matching.

It was never a dream; you had fallen ill, on a dirty floor,
now you are sane, after the pure absence, you twitch.

They avoid your touch, as your muscles tense, not with
anger, but in regret, you avoid your touch; you have
forgotten something.

The cleaners at the border took your keys,
the ones that lead outside the Gulags.

DO ZOBACZENIA

The strangers at the airport block your view,
    time's run out, you're leaving, baby blue.

Your last breaths, with lungs stained by local cigarettes,
        last steps in your flat, the final lift ride down.

    You see the ghosts of guests, friendships lost and found
a bittersweet mirage, feet in the sky, heads on the ground.

In your backpack - a one string violin,
with a mini whiskey bottle as it's donkey,
plays the saddest song ever composed,
as I step back and watch you go.

You hurry through the formalities,
the cliché goodbyes, security checks,
people forgotten how to walk or where to go,
nostalgia in limbo, until departure.

Then the views of home from above
create chaos in your thoughts,
all memories, good and bad,
begin to surface, a badly directed film.

The contradictions, the arguments,
the happier times, the walks at the docks,
late nights talking about art and music,
about lovers that took what they could
then left through the door.

Then the last part begins, when you arrive,
where you are expected despite delays,
people embrace you, they remember;
you have changed, but something stayed the same,
after the formalities, the process has finished.

When nostalgia takes over, and it will,
open a bottle of champagne to numb the pain.

Forget about us, forget about me,
       so that we can meet again.

The strangers at the airport block your view,
       time's run out, it's over, lonely you.

SHADOW OF A FRUIT

Taken from the teachings of the invisible guru,
on friendships and their shadows,
he adds me and you
and somehow ends up with 0.

This edition of LEVIATHAN contains the book

All Of This And Nothing

Some of the work is either drafts or initial ideas for the final poems in LEVIATHAN.

Unedited and raw, they represent the seeds of musings and melodies that were around at the time.

Also dedicated to friends and enemies.

All Of This And Nothing
Erik Davidkov

Published in the United Kingdom, 2017

for my mother

The pendulum of the mind oscillates
between sense and nonsense,
not between right and wrong.

C. G. Jung

I don't feel that it is necessary
 to know exactly what I am.
The main interest in life and work
 is to become someone else
that you were not in the beginning.

Michel Foucault

GOLDEN RATIO
an anfase of Katyusha

I have only seen it once, through the viewfinder
of your camera, and it was real, raw
and somewhat beautiful. Your curls, illuminated
by the red traffic light, your portrait -pale, freckled-
a smile not for my eyes, not this time, positioned
between the x and y, a symmetrical composition,
a tribute to Fibonacci. The backdrop – a wet Liverpool,
of course, burned on my retina, a 35mm negative of desire.

I often think of you and where you will be on photographs.

MACRORRHIZA
(from Latin) – a plant with large roots.

Through the window, I see my mother, kneeling in the garden,
her hands, opened wide, in conversation with God,
among flowers, roses, daffodils, a baby cherry tree,
all of them, including mother, encased in dirt, the roots.

I walk to her. I kneel next to my mother, hear voda, voda.
This is a prayer for water. She is kindly asking for water.
Not from God, she holds no idols close, but from Nature.

Nothing is better than bad weather. I surrender.

I see the sky, with its rain, dripping in my mouth,
like rain drips from a petal of a rose, onto its stem.
I touch the wet grass. It crackles between my fingers.
The sun is rising from the east. We are heliotropes.
I bury my feet into the soil, turn towards east.

I am a plant.

MARTYRDOM

Everything leads up to this,
Their hypocrisy, an act,
Their broken wings - a fertile zone,
On which insects breed.
Under a wing, in rotting flesh,
A malnourished zygote is formed.
Above the wing, a dance takes place. The swans
Entangle their necks in a noose-like structure,
Loose at the tip, tight at the base.
And it looks like a relic from old Berlin -
A white dada quartz pipe,
A boycott of the physical.
They kiss, their insects take lead.
Their Augustine feathers itch,
Their white necks detach, the physical-dismantled,
Cygnets gather, rich, next to mother,
Cobbe, fragile, at the centre of it all.
Trapped in a world that doesn't care about his song
Cobbe gargles an oil stain off the surface of the pond,
Clears his throat, spreads his wings, a bird in pain.
The feathers come off, he is Lazarus, and then,
Then the first and only song begins.
A crescendo - a hundred and forty piece
Orchestra and a choir of angels in the lungs -
A song about life, death and the importance of sleep.
An angel, carefully crafted by God,
With cold hard quartz snug around his heart,
A casualty of a long-fought war, sings.

LEMNISCATE FORMULA

Think of Schrödinger's cat.
Imagine you are Schrödinger's cat.
Think of time.
Think of infinity.

$$\infty + \infty = ?$$

Don't think too much about it.

DOES THE NOISE IN MY HEAD BOTHER YOU?
somewhat inspired by Pablo Picasso

In a plague of fantasies, apolitical and painful,
and a hundred and forty scenes of departure,
several (dis)figurations of the self are present.

At once, the painter sees himself as three different men.

I
A child, learning how to paint a house with geometry.

II
A young man, painting his naked girlfriend, who he calls either a goddess or a doormat.

III
An old man, looking for a paint tube that has not dried out yet.

There is a fourth (dis)figuration, only present at times of melancholy.

V
The painter sees himself as a piece of thread stuck between wax.
The thread burns, taking everybody down, the wax melts slowly.

1973 at his chateau near Cannes on the French Riviera.
The painter listens to a bluebird sing (or maybe cry) through the window of his room, where he lays on the bed he calls a catafalque.
On the floor, a letter, covered in different colours made of tears.

One more time with feeling.
All my life I have burned, but I never complained
    and I never called water to my rescue.
    Let the world turn, let it turn, it spins,
    it spins, it spins, without me,
    it spins, it spins
    no more.

MAE MONA

His shadow, burned onto film, an ever-fading memory
on a little boy's camera, on the other side of the cage.

His mother, though primitive, knew he was gone.
It was at that moment she realized, that the dead
weigh more than their own weight.

She would still feel his body in her arms,
as a baby, as a pre-pubescent ape, a cradle.

As night comes, the mother would put her child
on the ground, cover it with leaves and faint.

The dead weigh more than their own weight.
The heaviest ones are children.

EXPLAINING JOSEPH BEUYS
TO HIS DEAD HARE

The portrait is the grey felt suit.
It gives and receives emotion
and when nobody is looking
it moves and dances,
and translates poetry
in the wrong key.

VESSEL

Every time you sneeze
you don't think.
Every time you orgasm
you don't think.

All other times you think
and you don't even know.

CLEANING THE HOUSE

an old bouquet   left aside
and in between the lifeless petals -
a body of a moth with its neck snapped.
a china plate with an apple cut in half,
on its fourth day of oxidation, sings a song.
this is just an echo; the song comes from elsewhere.
the moth-   pyrite cube
an element forced upon its creator
an inverted silhouette,   the great beauty
waves the wrinkles off the surface
the doll-   benevolent object
with a child's complexion,
a marionette   perversely on top
a damp newspaper,   out of date,
coffee stains like freckles on the table,
looking for a meaning,   looking for water
this is the song that has never been written down,
a song of emotion, relation and the importance of sleep,
depicting a modern-day Prometheus.
its face -   an insect
dismissed from life,   from breath.
a song never sung,   it tries to hum.
the marionette whispers 5:15 to the moth:
and the prayer offered in faith will make the sick – well.
the pyrite cube crumbles   the wings fall off.
in the lungs   there is no hum.

L'ACCORD BLEU
after Yves Klein

The sky is as blue as I want it to be,
And, if I choose to believe grandmother,
then grandfather is up there,
dressed like a king of the wild frontier
with blue paint stains on his hip.
He flips pork loins on a grill
and listens to Lennon and McCartney,
throws bones for the dogs to fetch,
still reading Henning Mankell's novel,
lying in a hammock, counting planes,
thinking about how, when I was little,
I threw a Rolling Stones' record out the window,
and how it decapitated a pigeon.
Then he'd be thinking of me
and when I'd come home.

72 HOURS

I

In Belgrade, we lie on the grass,
the two of us, naked, like animals
our skins touch, like sand and glue.
Beetles in my stomach, butterflies in yours.

II

In the Sava lake we swim for hours,
our hands acquire a sea creature-like texture.
I touch your back, you turn around.
We breathe in deep and dive.

III

We kiss for an hour, then you walk away
and look for somebody else to set on fire.

CADMIUM RED
after John Berger and John Christie

For no better reason than to remind you of flowers,
I send you cadmium red. It is the same colour
of, say, when you were a child looking at the sky,
closing your eyes, seeing the blood in your eyelids,
that red, not violent as it can sometimes be,
but innocent, illuminated through the skin.
And say you opened your eyes, saw your grandfather
throwing a colourful ball for you to catch.
You were on a beach, or maybe in a forest,
where nothing is better than bad weather.
Your grandfather is younger, picking up flowers,
piece by piece; broken petals on lonely ground.
Then you saw the bees pollinating and one of them
landed on your hand, stung a crucifix into your skin.
He flicked it away, go, go and pollinate elsewhere,
the pain closed your eyes and now, now it's over,
he is no longer there, nor are the bees, no, you have grown
now,
for the time being, you are leaping over red petals,
much like that ritual he told you about when you were a kid,
where father and son, barefoot, dance over embers that
radiate intense amounts of heat long after the fire has been
extinct, somewhere in ancient Greece, or Thrace, where
cadmium red, in the form of a flower, lies on top of a cold,
forgotten monolith.

THE DESCENT

Some of us grew up,
some of us stayed the same,
some of us grew in numbers
and some of us have died again.

Some of us were born to die,
some of us to move away,
some of us to say the words
some of us can never say.

Some of us are born to sin,
some of us are left behind,
some of us search for love,
some of us will never find.

A SHORT STORY ABOUT THE MAN
WHOSE LOVE WORE FORBIDDEN COLOURS

My love wears forbidden colours,
so, they tried to silence me.
They cut my tongue.
Now, I only sing.

HESITANT REALISM

Do you remember
as kids, just kids,
our little kiss
underneath the weeping willow?

A wet painting
dripping curiosity
of adulthood,
smeared by our fragile hands.

No different
from the others –
naïve youths,
growing up.

We had one canvas,
two distinct colours,
two different paths,
to two different lives.

I always wonder
if the kids we once were
would be proud
of what we have become?

half-way and one step forward
to the point of no return

Printed in Great Britain
by Amazon

35733970R00052